SWANSEA
Revisited

by David Roberts

Published by Bryngold Books Ltd
100 Brynau Wood, Cimla,
Neath, South Wales SA11 3YQ.

BRYNGOLD BOOKS

Typesetting, layout, editing and
design by Bryngold Books
Copyright © Bryngold Books 2016.

ISBN 978-1-905900-44-2

www.bryngoldbooks.com

About the author

David Roberts

Swansaea Revisited continues the unique pictorial nostalgia journey that David Roberts unexpectedly embarked upon nearly two decades ago. This is his 19th book in successive years and once again its pages provide a home for a fresh and fascinating harvest of images. The series has been saluted as an incomparable look-back in time which captures the flavour and the feeling of the way the city once was. People, places and events all feature throughout the book's pages along with many more atmospheric glimpses of Wales' seaside city in years past.

Swansea Revisited is a worthy companion for the previous titles in this long-running series and with a rapid rate of change so visible across the city, it will ensure that what once was, will never be forgotten.

Looking across the River Tawe to the derelict Weaver and Company Ltd., building and some familiar hilltop landmarks beyond, mid-1970s.

A big thank you

Swansea Revisited is a book which we hope will once again bring much enjoyment to a great many people far and wide. It is the result of photographic contributions, large and small which capture some unique times from the city's past and allow it to be seen from a different perspective, often through the eyes of those who were there, camera in hand.

We are grateful for the support and involvement of: Hugh Rees, Peter Muxworthy, Peter Bailey, Ken and Marie John, John Murphy, Julie Jones, Kathryn Owens, Stephen Miles, Peter and Carol Nedin, Barry Griffiths, Tom Coleman, Clive Cockings, Marilyn Evans, Raymond and Dorothy Lewis, Hilary Evans, David Govier, Colin Andrew, Steve Davies, Jean Evans, Robert Davies, Roger Green, John Southard, Steve and Sandra McCulloch, Amanda Davies, Colin Riddle, Bill Morris, Keith Roberts, Gerald Lindenburn, Steve Philips, Dai Vaughan, John Roberts, Adeline Evans, Geoff Rees, Richard and Anne Evans, Mike Hallett, Bryndon J Evans, Diane Morgan, Bryn Evans, Sylvia and Bernard Miles, Louise Watkins, Eric Hill, Graham Davies, Barry Jones, Roger Fordham, Harry Geil, Bill Lumber, Roy Morgan, John Hughes, Charlotte Barry, Eddie Ford, Mrs Bryant, Sarah Hendra, Des and Diana Jones, Liz Sheldon, David Webborn, Raymond and Rion Davies, Richard Evans, JG Davies, Marilyn Hancock, Anne Howell, Idris Edwards, Phyllis Palmer and last, but certainly not least, the South Wales Evening Post.

Others without whose involvement **Swansea Revisited** – my 19th book on the city in as many years – would not have appeared include Charlie Wise, Neil Melbourne, David Beynon and Gerald Gabb. Lastly, but by no means least, I must thank my wife Cheryl for her unfailing support. Without that I am sure Swansea Revisited or indeed any of my books would never have appeared.

David Roberts

Share your pictures

If you have photographs of people, places or events in and around Swansea right up to recent times then you could play a part in the next Swansea nostalgia book. Please telephone 01639 643961 or e-mail david.roberts@bryngoldbooks.com to discover the ways in which you can do this. Only the involvement of people like yourself keeps this intriguing, long-running social record alive. All photographs, transparencies, negatives, black and white or colour, of people, places, events, streets, buildings, schooldays and sport are considered whatever their age or subject. They are all promptly returned. We can also receive your pictures electronically. Meanwhile, if you have missed any of the previous 18 books why not contact us now as some titles are still available to help complete your collection. You can also check out our many other similar titles at:

www.bryngoldbooks.com

Proud and passionate

THE story that is Swansea can be told in many ways, each and every one of which leads to the fact that it is experiencing an ever-increasing rate of change. Part of this must be attributed to the fact that the city has become a prime location on the global learning map, something evidenced by the cosmopolitan atmosphere created by those drawn to its excellent centres of learning from far and wide.

Visitors from across the oceans have however always played a part in life around the River Tawe and brought their own brand of change. From the earliest arrival of the Vikings and then the Normans, followed by Belgians, Italians and Germans to work in the metallurgical industries; the Irish and Devonians to work on the trams, Indians and Chinese to perhaps establish their individual taste experiences, all have helped shape what we are today. Most will welcome such an onward march, although some will at the same time, lament the passing of the old order. Perhaps this is understandable for it is the past that, after all, has provided the foundation for what is happening right here, right now and also what lies ahead. Others will mourn the fact that many visiting students will acquire new skills here and then head off to other lands. Hopefully they will spread the word about the Swansea experience.

The city should be proud of its progress through the early decades of the 21st Century despite the fact that its modern developments have rarely strayed too far from controversy and criticism. Past times have seen The Kingsway, High Street and Civic Centre occupy the spotlight. Before that it could have been anything from the demise of the Mumbles Railway to the building of the River Tawe barrage. There will also be those who love and those who hate the idea that turned Wind Street into a café quarter. Despite all of this and the coming — and then going — of its 'bendy buses' the city thrives and is the envy of many of its UK counterparts. No doubt its seaside location and Premier League football team play a part here.

Whatever the future may bring, Swansea people will continue to go about their daily lives proud and passionate about what they do and where they live. In quiet moments, as they sip a coffee or raise a pint of beer, they will continue to mull over the way things were before the latest change to demand their attention. Memories of the appearance of the city, its surroundings and the people who made it what it is will be evoked by the images on the pages of **Swansea Revisited**. Some of the subjects are just a few years old proving that it's as easy to pine for something that vanished yesterday as that which disappeared from the landscape decades before. It is also an indisputable pointer to the relentless pace of 21st Century change.

Hopefully the mix of pictures in this book will bridge the generations and help to detail the story that is Swansea for young and old; those who are Swansea born and bred as well as those who have just arrived and are getting to know their new home.

David Roberts, 2016.

A fascinating panorama of the mouth of the River Tawe, Swansea Docks and surrounding land, July 31, 1983. At this time Weaver's grain store had yet to be demolished to make way for Sainsbury's (Bottom right) and the mudbanks in the river reveal that the barrage was many years away. Industrial buildings proliferated on the wedge of land between the South Dock Marina and Swansea Beach including those of the Viscose and Spontex companies. Swansea's adopted Royal Naval vessel HMS Glamorgan can be seen berthed at King's Dock.

Captain Evans, minister of Cwm Mission, Cwm Road, Hafod, with some of its earliest members. He can be seen in the second row with a beard. The picture was probably taken around the time of the First World War.

A tram heads down Castle Bailey Street, into Wind Street, early 1900s.

Shoppers on the pedestrian crossing in lower High Street, outside the Woolworth store, May 1973.

Lord Mayor of Swansea, Councillor Lilian Hopkin MBE, attends a Social Service coffee evening at the Penlan Centre, June 1986. Sadly Councillor Hopkin died in April 2013.

Two of the tugs owned by the Alexandra Towing Company that were a familiar sight to vessels entering and leaving Swansea Docks during the early 1960s, await their next duty.

A carnival procession moves along Oxford Street, August 24, 2002.

Hazel Johnson with some of her younger School of Dancing members, all dressed up for an Easter performance, 1984.

Swansea tram No. 22 heads into Craddock Street from Mansel Street past the Albert Hall cinema on its way to the docks, mid-1930s. The tram just visible on the left is heading for High Street station from Sketty.

Boys and girls of Birchgrove Nursery School, with their teachers, 1964. The coping stones on the wall behind the group were made from copper waste.

The extension to the track of the Mumbles Railway towards the pier shortly after it opened, 1898.

Staff of South Wales Transport at the company's Ravenhill headquarters alongside WNO 484, fleet number 500, a 1953 open top, Bristol KSW5G double decker bus that was painted in a special silver livery to celebrate the Silver Jubilee of Queen Elizabeth II 1977.

Members of staff of the Lewis Lewis department store, High Street, during a trip to Llandrindod Wells, June 1962. They were in fancy dress for a competition which they won with their entry entitled Shotgun Wedding.

Complete with his Olympic tee-shirt and a big smile this youngster was delighted to pose for the camera against the post box at Swansea Marina, painted gold to salute the success of Swansea based swimmer Ellie Simmons in the 2012 Olympics.

Trevor Dawson of ET Dawson of Gwydr Square, Uplands, the last of the district's traditional grocery stores, 1963. He is pictured with a customer who won a national competition run by the Danish Bacon Company and supported by his promotional window display. The winner's prize was to have a house built and fully furnished. Both Trevor and the lucky winner were invited to Denmark as guests of the company. The winner's house was later built at Langland.

Pupils of Plasmarl School with teaching staff, 1956.

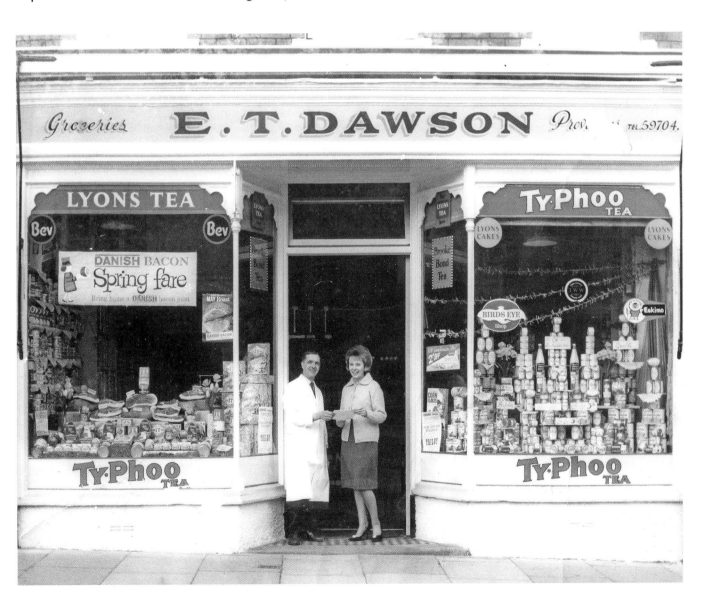

Dismantling work underway
on cranes near D shed,
King's Dock, late 1950s.

Members of Richard Thomas and Baldwins Landore works trip to Barry.

A family from Cadle Mill, complete with their dogs, enjoy a day out at Pwll Du Bay, Gower 1936.

Members and officials of Blaenymaes AFC with their mascot, December 12, 1994.

Farmworker Leonard Tomlin with a dapple grey mare in the yard of the farm at Singleton Park, 1952.

Crowds line St Helen's Road as floats entered in the 1971 Swansea Carnival parade pass by. This one was provided by well known, Llansamlet based haulier, Entress and won third prize in the Trade class.

Employees of the Hodges Menswear factory, Fforestfach Industrial Estate. 1951.

Vessels in the River Tawe at low tide in the mid-1980s, before construction of the barrage. Completed in 1992, it created a new marina at the mouth of the River Tawe, extending the leisure boat facilities already being offered by the former South Dock at that time.

A queue stretches along West Way on June 12, 1976. Those in its ranks were waiting to enter the Vetch Field for a concert headlined by world famous rock group The Who. The concert was part of its 'Who Put the Boot In' leg of their world tour, so called because they were gigs played at football stadiums. The image below captures the scene inside the Vetch during the concert.

A busy day at the Quadrant bus station, 1980s.
INSET: Passengers enter a Bristol VRT double decker while the boarded up concourse windows alongside conceal damage caused when a similar vehicle failed to stop and collided with the building after its brakes failed.

Aneurin Morgan with his wife outside
the boot and shoe repair shop he ran
in Carmarthen Road.

This view of The Palace theatre isn't
possible any longer. When it was taken all
the buildings around it had been
demolished to make way for new housing.

Members of the 36th Swansea (Sketty Wesley) Cub Scout pack with leaders, February 28, 1993.

Fuel pumps outside Fairwood Stores, Upper Killay, in 1920 with the staff who operated them.

Members of Swansea West Side All Stars comedy band, late 1980s.

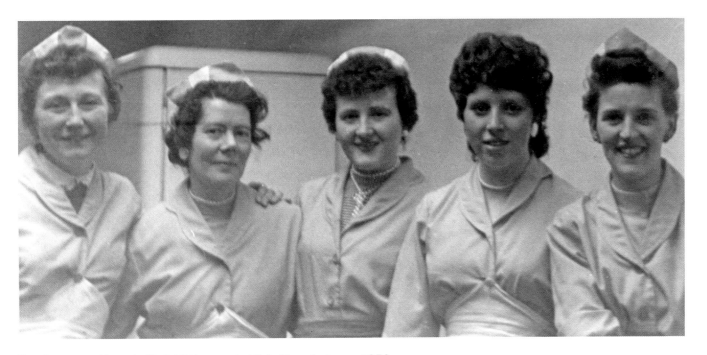

Food preparation staff at Littlewoods High Street store, 1959.

Staff of the Oxford Street store of Marks & Spencer at their annual dance at the Mackworth Hotel, High Street, 1937.

A group of friends at the Top Rank, Kingsway, during a specially arranged Thirties Night, late 1960s.

The covered grandstand at Morfa Stadium, Upper Bank, shortly before it was demolished in 2003 prior to construction across the River Tawe of the Liberty Stadium, home of Swansea City FC and The Ospreys rugby team. The eight lane, 400 metre, synthetic track was officially opened in September 1980 by Daley Thompson who won an invitation race.

Morfa regional athletic ground during its early days, before the stand was built, May 1981. Because of the hot weather the railway embankment alongside, consisting of compacted material, was smouldering for months and sand had been dumped on it to extinguish the fire.

A vessel leaves the South Dock marina on its way into the River Tawe and the sea during the early 1980s.

The Central Motors filling station in front of Westland Engine Supplies, Gowerton, late 1960s.

Two youngsters brave the chilly water of the outdoor paddling pool in Ravenhill Park, mid-1930s. The park was opened in 1931 after Lowe's farm was bought for £4,170.

Excavation work of the previously infilled South Dock and its basin appear to be nearly complete, allowing restoration work to begin before it was revitalised as a marina. The girder bridge spanning the link channel was later cut in half, with the surviving section still existing alongside the Pump House restaurant. The marina, which can accommodate nearly 400 boats, was officially opened in 1982.

Queens and their attendants prepare to take part in an Upper Killay carnival parade, early 1950s.

Looking up Newton Road, Mumbles, late 1950s.

A class of pupils and their teacher at Emmanuel Grammar School, 1953.

A group of young Penlan friends dressed in traditional Welsh costume on a sunny St David's Day, late 1950s.

A very quiet Gower Road, Upper Killay, early 1950s.

Staff enjoy a Christmas drink in the manager's office at the Unit Superheater works, The Strand, 1972.

Members of the committee of Longfields Centre, West Cross, 1979.

A day in the life of Cadle Mill farm, 1946.

The Bush Hotel,
Sketty Cross, 1984.

The Bonymaen Inn, Talfan Road, Bonymaen, mid-1970s. A South Wales Transport AEC Bridgemaster double decker is about to depart the bus stop and continue on route 80 to Morriston.

Jean's shop at the junction of High Street and Tontine Street once sold a tasty selection of faggots, pies and pastries, early 1970s.

The sprawling Morganite Electrical Carbon works at Upper Fforest Way, Morriston, late 1970s. In the years that have passed, it has been significantly reduced in size and much of the left hand side of its expanse is now the site of the town's Asda store.

Three drivers who were employed by British Road Services at the company's North Dock depot in front of a contract vehicle operated by the company for Bottogas Services, 1962.

Two young friends from Soar Chapel Sunday School, Dyfatty, about to board the Swan Motor Company single deck AEC Regal coach that carried them on a Whitsun excursion, 1951.

The Dunvant RFC squad for the 1993-1994 season seen with club officials.

The sign on the cart says Pure Ices and that's exactly what it brought to the people of Cadle Mill, Fforestfach, during the late 1930s. The ice cream was made by the cart's Italian owners.

Signalmen inside Burrows Sidings signal box, June 1987.

Friends and relatives of Swansea couple Mr & Mrs Dymond join them to help celebrate their Diamond Wedding, June 14, 1952.

Vessels at King's Dock, early 1960s.

Looking across the rooftops towards the
River Tawe and the docks, mid-1980s.

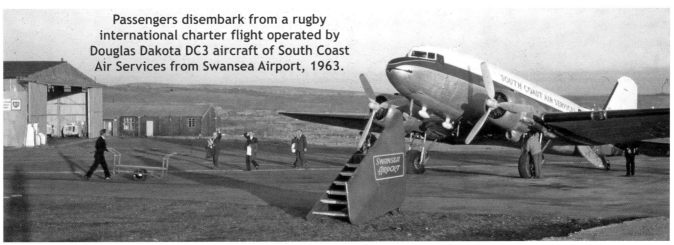

Passengers disembark from a rugby
international charter flight operated by
Douglas Dakota DC3 aircraft of South Coast
Air Services from Swansea Airport, 1963.

Pupils of a class at Llwchwr Infants School, with teaching staff, 1955.

Robert Milliner and Florence Evans, with guests at their Swansea wedding, April 1943.

Neighbours who lived in prefabs at Llanelli Place, Fforesthall, enjoy a chat, early 1950s.

Mrs F Roberts cleaning Cwm Mission, Hafod, which she did on a regular basis. The mission was originally a part of St John's Church, and was destroyed by bombing during the Second World War. It re-opened at the end of Cwm Road, near the Lower Compass public house on Llangyfelach Road.

A mother with her two children at Treboeth on St David's Day, 1953.

The Glynn Webb home improvement warehouse at Fforestfach, February 16, 2002.

Members of Tirdeunaw Welsh School Folk Dance Team 2011.

The 12.10pm, Saturdays only, Pontarddulais to Swansea Victoria all stations train waits at Swansea Bay station, alongside Mumbles Road, before proceeding to its destination, early 1960s. The stand of St Helen's rugby and cricket ground is in the background.

Looking over Swansea Castle and Castle Gardens, from the top of the BT Tower, July 1973.

Work begins on construction of the Wind Street pedestrian subway, May, 1965. Like the railway bridge across the entrance to Wind Street, it has now vanished.

Prefects of Oystermouth Secondary School, mid 1950s.

The Cwmbwrla Cheery Boys with friends, in front of the hut where they met every week in Cwmbwrla Park.

A trainload of imported Australian coal for Aberthaw Power Station hauled by a class 66 locomotive, snakes its way across the remains of the railway network at Swansea Docks on an overcast, January 18, 2001.

The 16.15pm train from Swansea Victoria to Pontarddulais passes under the footbridge at Swansea Bay station, April 4, 1963.

A group of members of Soar Sunday School on a Whitsun trip to Llandeilo.

Residents of Bath Avenue and Bath Road in Morriston, during the party they held to celebrate the end of the Second World War in a small nearby field.

Gwyrosydd Junior School teacher
Mrs Jenkins and headteacher Mr
Sinnett with a class of pupils, 1960.

Staff at BT Telecom's tower block, The Strand, take a break, 1968.

The Shell Tankers oil carrier Fragumis, eased through the lock at Swansea Docks, before berthing at the Queen's Dock oil terminal to discharge her cargo, May 9, 1960.

Mr & Mrs Stephen Vaughan with their son David, alongside a 1948 Bristol 33-seat coach bought from Silcox Motors, Pembroke Dock for £75 in 1961. It was used by 1st Swansea YMCA Scout troop for many years.

The large floral clock at Victoria Park, early 1920s.

Traffic on Carmarthen Road, Dyfatty, late 1970s.

A view over Bonymaen, mid-1960s. Skewen and the Neath Valley can be seen in the distance.

A National Bus Company South Wales single deck bus passes a sister vehicle heading out of the city centre in Dyfatty Street, as it conveys Park and Ride passengers into Swansea from Landore, during December 1980.

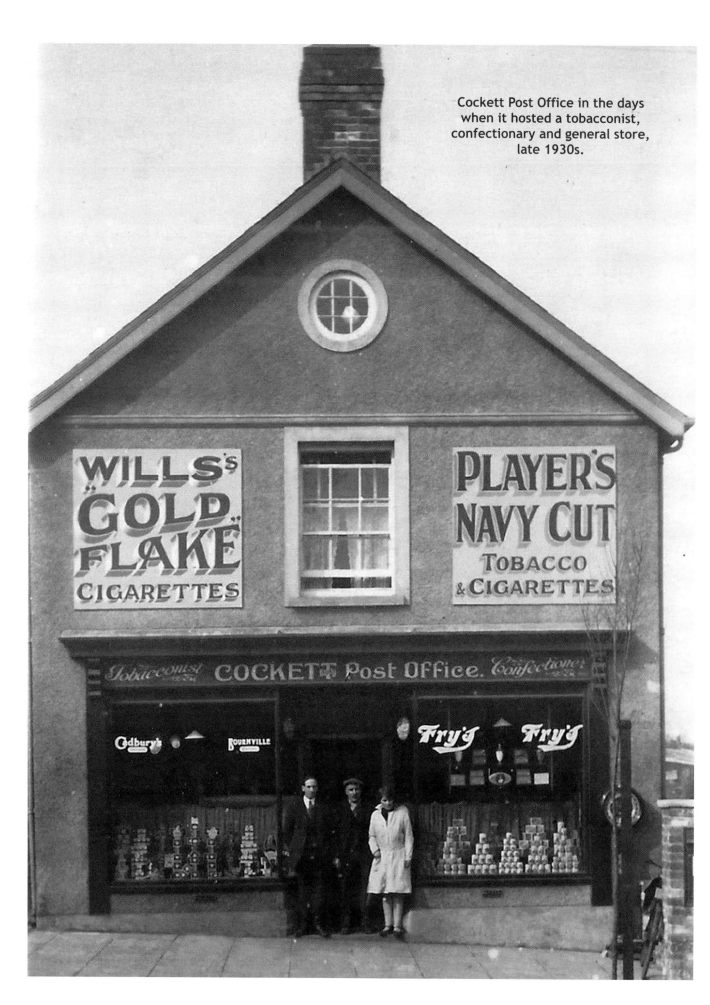

Cockett Post Office in the days when it hosted a tobacconist, confectionary and general store, late 1930s.

It looks as though the local fishing fleet had landed a good catch before this snapshot of the fish market at Swansea Docks was captured in the late 1930s.

Looking from the roof of the Grand Theatre towards Clarence Terrace and in the background, West Glamorgan County Hall, late 1980s. Swansea prison is on the right.

Looking across High Street station towards St Thomas, May 24, 1985. This view from one of the upper floors of the Land Registry building, shows Unit Superheater works and its neighbour, both now vanished.

Pupils of Form 1B Danygraig Secondary Modern School, 1960.

Staff at work in the model shop at the Louis Marx toy factory, Fforestfach, early 1960s.

Members of Swansea West Side All Stars Comedy Band horsing around in a 1967 carnival parade.
In those days, so the price on the pump tells us, petrol was just five shillings and seven pence a gallon.
That's just about 28 pence today, when a gallon costs around £5.25p!

Swansea women, June and Rion Lewis, show off the latest fashions in coats, gloves and handbags on the steps of The Slip bridge, early 1950s.

Gerald Fussell, proprietor of Fussell's coaches, stands proudly in front of one of the company's Bedford coaches, mid 1970s.

The Dragon Hotel, The Kingsway, takes centre stage in this bird's eye view,
with the former Swansea Fire Station in the background, right, and Dynevor School, left, 1973.

The arrival at King's Dock of the 12,398 ton Havdrill, a specially built ocean bed drilling vessel attracted plenty of attention during, June 1974. Built in 1973 it was equipped with a series of propellors to hold her in position while drilling. Her name was changed several times until in 2010 she was renamed Jasper Explorer.

Gower Road, Sketty, was a much quieter thoroughfare in 1910, as these people walking in the centre of the road prove.

Fforestfach Post Office obviously sold a range of other wares as the displays in its front windows in the late 1930s shows.

Seen in 1970, this is the rotting hulk of a sailing vessel alongside the Pockett's Wharf jetty near the South Dock entrance that was used by paddle steamers. This is near the entrance to today's South Dock Marina.

Four of Phyllis Jones's Swansea Babes dancers who took part in the pantomime Jack and the beanstalk, staged at the Grand Theatre, 1955.

Vessels lay in the mud of the River Tawe at low tide before construction of the barrage, mid-1980s.

Swansea City fans queue at the turnstiles for one of the club's home games during the 1986-87 season. Others have already taken their seats as this view of Vetch Field, from the roof of the Grand Theatre shows.

Police Constable Jack Owen at his desk in Sketty Police Station, late 1950s.

Two views of the main pool at Swansea Leisure Centre shortly before it was opened by Queen Elizabeth II, September 1977, her silver jubilee year. The centre became one of the most popular tourist attractions in Wales and the pool's waters would seldom be as tranquil as this, particularly when its wave generator was in operation, as it attracted around 800,000 users annually until it closed for reconstruction in 2003.

Major improvement work, including the construction of a new larger stage and new dressing rooms, underway at the Grand Theatre, May 1984.

The creation of the Maritime Quarter had yet to begin when this mid-1970s scene, looking across the South Dock towards the pump house building, was captured.

Members of the 18th Swansea St Stephen's and 35th Danygraig Scout troops at summer camp,
Builth Wells, July, 1960.

Bonymaen Youth football team which took on East Side Colts in a league cup final at Vetch field, 1960.

Beach huts and the top of the shelter at Rotherslade Bay viewed from the Osborne Hotel, September 1993. Neither hotel nor the shelter now remain.

Chris Hutchings gets the ball away from a scrum during Dunvant RFC's encounter on September 2, 1995.

Some of those who participated in a 1980s Ostreme fete at Mumbles.

The United Carbon Black works, that stood alongside Fabian Way, Port Tennant, during demolition, 1972.

The hulk of a former Second World War Royal Navy motor torpedo boat which was moored on the shoreline at Norton, Mumbles for some years being investigated by a curious youngster, 1954.

David Thomas, left, a farm owner at Mynydd Newydd, Penlan, on a bench at Mynydd Newydd Common with two friends, and a canine companion, mid-1960s.

Looking down on a busy Oxford Street, on April 13, 1992. At the time all traffic had to turn right here into Upper Union Street, except buses which could continue straight through the junction.

Blackpill Lido, which offered both boating and paddling opportunities on warm summer days, late 1960s.

Shops at Graiglwyd Square, Townhill, mid-1950s.

Looking up High Street towards the station, early 1980s. King's Lane is on the right.

Some of the people who occupied Mayhill Farm, Townhill, early 1900s.

Construction of Swansea Council's depot at Pipe House Wharf, Morfa Road, nears
completion. BELOW: The interior of the arch-roofed building.

Often spotted in the skies over Swansea and surrounding areas these two balloons, pictured in the late 1970s, reflected the passion for getting airborne of Swansea Builders merchants proprietor DA Legg. The company was known as DAL the builder's pal and also had involvement with Fforestfach Greyhound Stadium.

Looking across railway sidings and Fabian Way at Port Tennant towards the Aluminium Wire and Cable Company's works in the mid-1980s. Behind are the oil storage tanks of BP.

Some of the dancers who delighted packed audiences at the Grand Theatre during the staging of the pantomime Aladdin, staged between December 13, 1958 and February 14, 1959. They are seen with one of the leading cast members. The girls were know as Phyllis Jones's Swansea Babes.

Some of the pupils who attended Cila School in 1965, with headmaster Mial Davies.

A group of busmen pose in front of a Swan Motors Leyland vehicle before making the return journey from a summer coach trip, late 1940s.

Oystermouth Castle, viewed from Newton Road, 1970.

There was plenty of work for these two Class 08
diesel locomotives at Kings Dock exchange
sidings on January 29, 1987.

A horse drawn brewery dray which was used to deliver products produced by WM. Hancock & Co Ltd to Swansea hostelries, during the 1950s. The brewery's stables were in Little Wind Street.

The paddling pool at Ravenhill Park, Fforestfach, late 1930s. Local authority housing had by this time started springing up in the fields that once lay close by. These homes are some of the first built at Fforesthall.

The Killay and Dunvant RFC 1948-1949 season squad with officials of the club.

Pupils of Brynhyfryd Infants School with their teacher and headteacher, 1985.

Some of the participants in
Mumbles carnival, 1976
aboard their float at
Bracelet Bay car park.

A bowls match underway at the Welfare Club rink of Richard Thomas and Baldwin's Landore and Dyffryn works mid-1980s.

St David's shopping centre, part of which for a time was home to a TV studio for S4C, 1992.

Properties in Carmarthen Road, above Dyffaty crossroads, shortly before they were demolished to make way for dual carriageway improvements, 1975. This view was taken from the end of Waun Wen Terrace.

Ivor the engine at the annual summer fete organised for employees of the Ford Motor Company's Swansea plant at Jersey Marine, 1976.

A view along Oxford Street as work progresses on Swansea's new post-war market in 1961. It had taken more than 20 years to replace the building destroyed by bombing during the Three Nights' wartime blitz.

Demolition work underway at the Midland railway station, St Thomas, during the construction of the Fabian Way dual carriageway into Swansea, 1960.

The stand of Swansea Rugby and Cricket Club's St Helen's ground dominates this view of traffic on Mumbles Road, late 1980s.

Passengers boarding a train at Swansea Victoria Station, late 1920s.

Crowds throng a bustling
High Street, during the 1970s.

Looking over the city
from Windmill Terrace,
St Thomas, early 1970s,
a skyline scene much
changed today.

Laura and Robert Miles at Vetch Field after Swansea City
Football Club had played its last match there, May 2005.

Danygraig Junior School's second year football squad, with their teacher and coach, October 1980.

A group of office, driver and dairy staff of Unigate Dairies, Hafod, with accountant Paul Leaman at a farewell function, 1994.

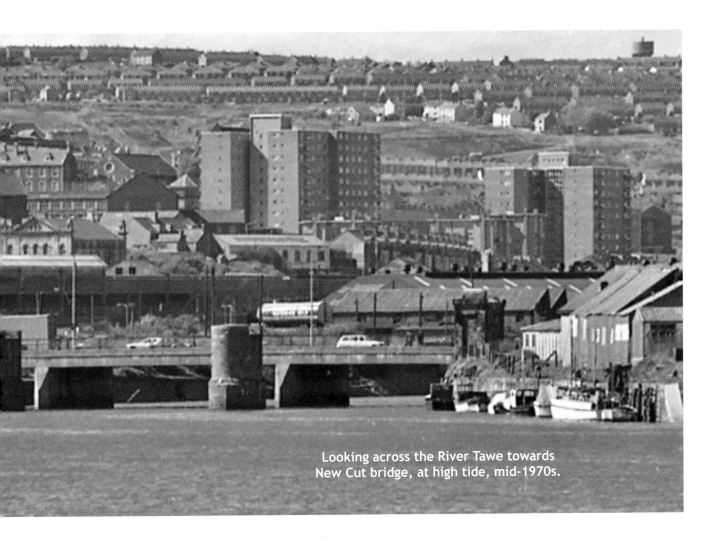

Looking across the River Tawe towards
New Cut bridge, at high tide, mid-1970s.

Victoria Evans and Harry Moore of Middle Road, Fforestfach with guests at their wartime wedding, 1942.

The Pearl Assurance building at The Kingsway and the floral oasis that was the roundabout at the thoroughfare's eastern end, mid-1950s.

The Green at Murton, Gower, 1947.

Members of the British Telecomm sales team who worked at Telephone House, The Kingsway, 1960.

The Princess Way elevation of the popular David Evans department store on February 11, 2004.
The '70 per cent off' clearance posters are a sad sign of its impending closure.

Rail tank wagons awaiting repair work alongside the United Carbon Black works, Port Tennant, late 1970s.

Opened in 1959, this was Swansea Central Fire Station, Grove Place, in the mid-1980s. The site now houses Swansea Central Police Station, the area headquarters for the Western Division of South Wales Police.

An atmospheric snapshot of Swansea Victoria Station, towards the end of its life, June 13, 1963. Standard Class 5 73097 locomotive has just arrived with the 12.00 train from Shrewsbury.

The Great Western Hotel, High Street, a landmark for anyone arriving in the city by train, September, 1973.

A St Thomas wedding, 1930s style.

Members of Morriston and District Nursing Association gathered outside Maes y Gwernen House, on July 7, 1923 with friends to celebrate its 21st anniversary. The ivy is now gone but the building still remains, close to all of the modern buildings visible today at Morriston Hospital. Back row: WJ Webber, D Jeremy, G Bowen, WJ Walters, D Morgan, Jno Jones, J John, W Buckland, Cllr WJ Davies JP, Reverend G Thomas, Vicar; Third row: J Bridle, nurse Edmonds, nurse Lewis, Mrs AR Lewis, Mrs Jas Jones, Mrs L Richards, Mrs William Davies, Mrs Ed. John, Mrs McMinn, London; Miss Dudley, Mrs Walter Williams, Mrs David Harris, chairman of guardians; Second row: nurse Megan Williams, W Lewis JP, Mrs TH Jones, Tom Davies, chairman of comittee; Lady Edwards, vice president; Mrs TJ Williams, president; TR Williams, honorary secretary; AR Lewis, William Davies, nurse Margaret Williams. Front row: W Harris, Guardian J Griffths, B George, Mrs G Thomas, Miss Valerie Edwards, Master Clive Edwards, Miss Gwyneth Williams, Mrs DM Davies and WJ Price.

The flattened remains of Sketty Primary School, Tycoch Road, after it was demolished to make way for a new housing complex, 2015.

A gathering of Thyssen workers engaged in the construction of the Quadrant Shopping Centre as they near the end of their involvement in what remains the principal undercover shopping mall in the city. The centre opened in 1979 and has a floor area of 440,000 sq ft.

A group of Swansea dockers enjoy a well-earned tea break, mid-1950s.

Swansea market traders present a cheque to Dilys Bailey, the chairman of the Longfields Association's West Cross centre for the disabled, to help boost its funds and further its aims, 1980s.

Members and officials of the bowls team at the Landore works of Richard Thomas & Baldwin with the trophy that resulted from a successful season, late 1950s.

Pupils who took part in Bishop Gore School's production of the play Norah, hard at work behind the scenes early 1960s.

The tug Clyneforth escorts the lightship Helwick into Swansea Docks for maintenance work, mid-1960s.

Construction of the Holiday Inn hotel, which later became the Swansea Marriot, Trawler Road, in the Maritime Quarter, late 1980s.

The opening of the new Co-operative Food convenience store at Tycoch Square, March 2015.

Looking across the Carrot Pond, Gors Avenue — so-called because of its shape — and the rooftops of Cwmbwrla, 1990s. The pond was a reservoir for the nearby Richard Thomas and Baldwin's works.

The lock entrance to Swansea Docks, 1962, with some interesting construction work going on alongside.

Players and officials of Cwm Wanderers AFC, with the spoils of a successful season, May 1, 1991.

Some of the members of the Richard Thomas and Baldwins Landore works bowls team.

Looking down on the foyer of Swansea Civic Centre, 2015.

A group of members of Cwm Mission, Hafod, late 1950s. Among them on the far right is Desmond Roberts, who could often be seen giving out leaflets at the Union Street entrance of Swansea Market on a Saturday.

Children of workers at Richard Thomas and Baldwin's Landore works enjoy the entertainment at a Christmas party, late 1950s.

The panoramic view eastwards from the top of the Guildhall clock tower, mid-1980s. In the foreground is the former St Helen's tram depot with its offices on the left. It is now the site of Swansea Crown Court.

Looking towards Byron and Shelley Crescents, Mayhill, now named Long Ridge and High View, early 1960s.

Shops at Fforestfach Cross, early 1930s.

Young participants in a Christmas concert at Llangyfelach Primary School, December 9, 2015.

A South Wales Transport bus heading for Mumbles passes under the bridge that carried the LMS railway over the road and Mumbles Railway line at Blackpill, early 1920s.

A class of pupils at Dunvant Secondary Modern School with their teacher, 1962.

Members of Swansea West Side All Stars Comedy Band take a break from their capers during a carnival parade, 1967.

Looking across derelict land at the South Dock towards the original Swansea Leisure Centre, early 1980s.

Young members of the Hazel Johnson School of Dance, including Catherine Zeta Jones, in the checked hat, fifth from left in the third row back, early 1980s.

Some of the employees at the Landore works of Richard Thomas and Baldwins who helped prepare one of its successful annual children's Christmas parties, late 1950s.

The roads of Cockett carried far less traffic when this mid-1920s scene was captured.

The Upper Bank, Pentrechwyth transport depot of bus, coach and plant hire operators Morris Bros, mid-1980s. The site became a housing development in 2015.

Looking down Oxford Street from Princess Way, early 1960s.

Looking along Princess Way towards the Kingsway traffic roundabout, 1955. There were still terraced houses in Orchard Street at the time. This most popular of Swansea department stores was closed and eventually demolished in 2007. BELOW: A similar view, around two decades later in the mid-1970s.

A group of Swansea schoolchildren take time out from their celebrations to mark the Silver Jubilee of Queen Elizabeth II in 1977 to pose for the photographer.

Some of the staff, including doctors and nurses, of the former RAF hut at Upper Killay, which was used as a baby clinic for some years, 1946.

A group of Morriston schoolchildren
and their teachers seen during a
visit to the Houses of Parliament,
London 1978.

The 35 pupils of Standard 6B at Cwm Council School, with their teacher, 1925.

A South Wales Transport Leyland double decker, heading for Port Tennant on route 76, picks up what looks like a full load of passengers in Castle Bailey Street, outside the Castle buildings occupied by the South Wales Evening Post newspaper, 1951. Eddershaws, the family run business advertised on the side of the bus first opened for business in 1835 and closed its Swansea store in April 2013. This was followed in July 2016 by the closure of its Cardiff branch.

This was one of the Garrett steam lorries used by wholesale fruiters and potato merchants Batcup & Harries to deliver their wares across the city during the 1920s.

British Road Services lorries at the company's North Dock depot, 1960s.

The final days of the last surviving Mumbles Railway car. Tram No. 2 had been saved by the Middleton Railway, Leeds, for preservation, but neglect, vandalism and finally a fire resulted in it being scrapped in the late 1960s.

This 1955 panorama of Swansea city centre shows how it was finally rising from the ashes nearly a decade and a half after wartime bombing had all but levelled it. Though much rebuilding had taken place the market still remained an outdoor operation and the current building wasn't opened until 1961. The Dragon Hotel had also yet to be built at this time.

Some of the pupils of Killay Council School, 1915.

Swansea bride and groom Albert and Lucy Athernought with guests at their wedding, 1940.

Nurses and patients in a ward at the Swansea YMCA building which was put to use as a military hospital during the First World War, March 1919. Despite the month, Christmas decorations are still very much in evidence. BELOW: The Gym Ward at the YMCA, February 1918, a year earlier.

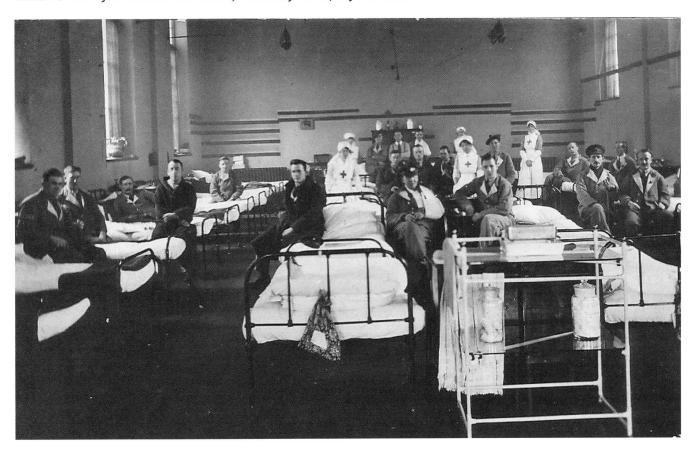

Members of Swansea Schoolboys' Under 15 football squad which included a number of Welsh capped players, together with officials at the end of the 1988-89 season.

These larger than life Disney cartoon characters proved a big hit with youngsters at the Quadrant Shopping Centre in 1981.

Pupils of Trallwn Primary School with their teacher Mrs Griffiths, 1986.

Staff of John Jones' Mumbles Dairy 1950.

Looking across the Kingsway roundabout into Princess Way, mid-1960s.

Verdi's ice cream parlour, Knab Rock, on a sunny summer's day, early 1990s.

Not a vehicle of any kind in sight — this was tree-lined Walter Road, in the much more tranquil times of 1903.

The MV Celtic Pride, one of the Swansea Cork Ferries vessels which operated a regular roll-on roll-off service linking the two cities, between 1987 and 2006, seen setting off on another sailing, September 1987.

A fascinating glimpse back in time at one of the parts of Swansea that has perhaps changed more than most in the past half a century. Seen in 1972, it clearly shows that work was well underway to fill in the South Dock basin and the channel that linked it to the South Dock itself. Shortly after the task was completed, work began to dig it out again to create today's modern marina. On the left here, the industrial scene has changed totally to be replaced by housing and an enhanced promenade. Any other hint of industry visible has also almost certainly given way to housing or marina development.

Houses in New Orchard Street shortly before demolition, September 1973.

Staff of Ward 5, Singleton hospital, Christmas 1976.

Looking into Norfolk Street from Terrace Road with the vertigo inducing drop into the playground of Terrace Road School on the right. Not much has changed since this picture was taken in 1976.

Parked cars near Sketty Cross, 1960s.

A train to Shrewsbury, via the Central Wales line, prepares to leave Swansea Victoria station, early 1960s.

With the pier and the old lifeboat house in the distance a Mumbles Railway car rattles and rolls its way along the foreshore at Southend, late 1950s.

Timber-built holiday bungalows dotted around the hillside at Limeslade, 1946.

Looking from South Road, alongside Swansea baths towards The Slip and Mumbles Road, mid-1980s.

A youngster enjoys a game of peek-a-boo on Mumbles Pier, during the summer of 1956.

The sweep of Swansea Bay
viewed from the Civic Centre
during construction
1982. The building originally
housed the headquarters of
West Glamorgan County Council.

Young footballers
at Lonlas Junior
School, 1972.

Committee members of the
Electrical Trades Union at the
Trades Union Congress,
held in the city, 1928.

The sprawling Velindre Tinplate Works, 1972. It was opened in 1956 to complement the facilities at Port Talbot's giant steel making plant. A decision to close the works was taken in 1980, redundancies were announced the following year and production ceased in 1989.

Flattened Swansea city centre begins to emerge from the ravages of aerial bombardment during the Second World War. This was the scene in the early 1950s.

Cooling lollipops for these women taking a break in the sunshine at Fforestfach, 1951.

Construction work underway on the River Tawe barrage, 1989.

Prior to the city becoming the destination for Wales' National Waterfront Museum, Swansea's own Maritime and Industrial Museum resided on this spot, as seen on November 17, 2002.

Swansea observatory, on the promenade at the Marina, 2002. It was originally home to Wales' largest optical astronomical telescope. The building was designed by Robin Campbell in 1989 and consists of two towers. From 1993 to Feb 2010 it was loaned to the Swansea Astronomical Society but returned to the hands of Swansea City Council. After remaining empty for some time since then, it has since been sold and is set for a new lease of life as a holiday home, cafe and gallery.

Highmead Avenue, Newton, after
overnight snow, January 1985.

The centre of Swansea was just a flat and open space until rebuilding began after the bombing the city had endured during the Second World War. This was Princess Way at its junction with Oxford Street, in 1952, with The Kingsway in the background.

Competitors completing the 2008 Swansea Bay 10k run.

Christmas shoppers in Oxford Street, 1982.

A shopper in Oxford Street, early 1960s.

A family at the entrance to Mumbles Pier, Easter Monday, 1968. Dad is probably behind the camera!

The sail bridge that spans the River Tawe, reflected in its waters, 2008.

Looking across the city from Townhill, over the SA1 development and the docks towards Port Talbot, 2007.

A group of young men from the Hafod and Townhill areas, February, 1958 following the fashion of the Teddy Boy era.

Looking across the South Dock towards the former Maritime and Industrial Museum, mid-1980s. The original Swansea Leisure Centre can be seen on the left. Much development has taken place in this area.

Looking down Newton Road, Mumbles, late 1970s. Morris and Ford vehicles seem to have been the favourites of the day.

A South Wales Transport AEC Regent V double decker bus heads into the city centre along The Kingsway on a wet afternoon during the mid-1970s.

An atmospheric, but very sad, nightime view of firemen tackling a blaze that destroyed the Grade II listed Libanus Chapel, Cwmbwrla. The fire was discovered at around 4.20am on January 21, 2012. At its height more than 50 firefighters were engaged in tackling the incident.

Two young girls enjoy playing in a tin bath in the back garden of their Fforestfach home, 1938.

The Bay View Hotel occupies centre stage in this view eastwards along Oystermouth Road, mid 1970s.

Some of the pupils of Swansea Secondary Technical School for girls, 1959-1960.

Construction of one of the
first buildings of the new
SA1 development, 2007.

Brandishing special tokens, these people were queuing in Townhill Community Centre for free butter and cheese as the government attempted to reduce a huge surplus in its emergency supply.

Gladys Lewis at work in the shop she ran alongside her house in Cadle Mill, late 1950s. Known as Cadle Mill Stores it started with just 12 customers and ended up with 350, mainly residents of the nearby housing estate.

Pupils and teachers at Cila School, Killay, gather to celebrate the Coronation of Queen Elizabeth II, June 1953.

The Commercial Inn, Plasmarl, 1976.

Looking along Cwm Level Road, from Brynhyfryd towards Plasmarl, 1960s.

Part of one of the popular Morriston Carnival parades, mid-1960s.

Construction of Swansea's first purpose-built multilateral school, the forerunner of comprehensive schools. Opened in 1956, as Penlan Multilateral School, it closed in 2001 after which it was refurbished before re-opening as Ysgol Gyfun Gymraeg Bryntawe, a Welsh medium comprehensive, in 2003.

Looking across Oystermouth Road towards Swansea Gasworks site that is now home to the Tesco Marina store. In the background the arched roof of the city's market can be seen.

Members and officials of Bonymaen rugby club, 1931-32. At the time they had been unbeaten at home for three seasons.

Looking prim and proper and presenting a riot of springtime colour, this was Castle Gardens, mid-1950s.

Cast members of the 1992, production of Snow White and the Seven Dwarfs, made up of students from all departments of the Llwyn-Y-Bryn campus of what is now Gower College, Walter Road.

Shops in High Street, opposite High Street railway station. The Tivoli Amusements building was formerly occupied by the James Bros drapery.

Members of the congregation of Mount Calvary Church, Danygraig, during a Nativity production, late 1940s.

Principal guests at the marriage of Ivor Rees to Olive Jenkins in Manselton on February 8, 1936.

An interesting night-time panorama over Swansea with fireworks in the sky and the lights of Port Talbot just visible across the bay, 2010.

The Lewis Lewis department store occupies centre stage in this view up High Street towards the railway station, mid 1950s.

A group of young St Thomas boys make some running repairs to the home made gambo that had no doubt provided them with hours of fun and excitement on the hilly streets of the area, May 1960.

A group of engineering staff at the Ravenhill main depot of the South Wales Transport bus company, early 1960s.

A group of Pontarddulais residents who gathered to celebrate VE Day, 1945.

A sad day for the postmistress at Upper Killay for 49 years — the date was June 29, 2013 and it was her last day at the helm.

Alongside the Bedford coach that carried them on the day trip that was a welcome break from their daily labours, are these smartly dressed employees of the Landore works of steelmakers Richard Thomas and Baldwins. They were heading off for a day at the races, late 1950s.

This crowd of people from Swansea and the surrounding area, were enjoying a paddle steamer trip across the Bristol Channel to Ilfracombe in the early 1950s.

Looking seawards along Paxton Street, across Oystermouth Road and under the two rail bridges, early 1950s.

Part of the busy British Road Services, North Dock depot, early 1960s.

A Cambrian Airways Viscount aircraft at Swansea Airport, 1967.

Grenfell Park Road, St Thomas, 1973.

Crowds flock to the banks of the River Loughor for a regatta, mid-1930s.

The gardens at Southend and behind, the attractive facade of the Mermaid Hotel, July 1984.

164

The Meridian Tower slowly rises over neighbouring buildings on the seafront promenade at the Marina, overlooking Swansea Bay, March 19, 2008.

Swansea City football legend Ivor Allchurch with Cwm Albion's carnival team, during celebrations to mark the Coronation of Queen Elizabeth I, June 1953.

Hordes of competitors in the annual Mumbles fun run, 1982.

A fascinating view of walkers working off the excesses of Christmas fare on Worm's Head, Gower, December 28, 2008.

Members of the congregation of Terrace Road Chapel, Mount Pleasant, on their annual Whitsun outing to Dunvant Park, May 25, 1953.

Washing sheep at Carter's Ford, Gower, late 1940s.

Employees of the Swansea office of the Co-operative Insurance company on a day out, 1958.

Workmen put the finishing touches to the pedestrian subway at the top of the Kingsway at its junction with Princess Way, College Street, Orchard Street and Belle Vue Way, January 1, 1974.

The Dragon Hotel towers over the now vanished Kingsway pedestrian underpass, 1985.

A Standard Class 4, 2-6-4T, locomotive 80069, leaves Swansea Victoria station, on June 20, 1963, heading the 16.15 local train to Pontarddulais.

A South Wales Transport AEC Regent III double decker waits for its cargo of passengers to leave the beach at Caswell Bay and jump aboard for their journey home on route 40 which was headed for Morriston.

With most of its roofing stripped, this was the former Cwmfelin tinplate works in 1985.

Guests during a presentation that formed part of a Swansea Ambulance Service retirement dinner at the Dolphin Hotel, late 1960s.

Foxhole Road, Foxhole, St Thomas, 1973.

Landore locomotive depot drivers Ray Voisey and Roger Moss, changing over as caretakers for two steam locomotives temporarily stationed there. The locomotives had been working in Fishguard that Saturday and Sunday. Number 6000 King George V and 7029 Clun Castle both played a prominent part in the Great Western Railway's 150th anniversary celebrations, 1985.

Upper Killay Cricket XI with their mascot, mid-1980s.

The reception class at Manselton Infants School, with their teacher, 1991.

Magnet Club mixed darts team members who were winners of the Morriston Hospital Darts League, 1954.

This group of stately ladies are about to set off on a day trip, courtesy of the Gower Vanguard bus company, in the mid-1930s.

Campers pitched up at Horton, Porteynon, early 1930s.

Properties awaiting
demolition in Oxford
Street, early 1980s.

Youngsters enjoy the fine fare on offer at a party organised in Margaret Street, St Thomas,
to celebrate the Investiture of the Prince of Wales, July 1969.

Children on the roundabout in the playground, at Jersey Park, St Thomas, 1962. In the background children are queuing up for a drink at the water fountain!

Children from Prior's Way, Dunvant, on a float built by Viv Evans, who was a window dresser for the Co-operative, and which was entered in Dunvant Carnival parade, 1980.

Three youngsters in Harbour View Road,
overlooking Jersey Park, St Thomas,
pose for the photographer, 1958.

Police Sgt Willis, a traffic policeman at one of the cycling proficiency courses he organised at the Drill Hall, Richardson Street, Sandfields, every Saturday, in the late 1950s.

Members of East Side Historical Society 1998.

Employees of the British Fuel Company, Gloucester Place during a Christmas dinner, early 1980s.

A First Cymru ftr metro 'bendy bus' battles with the traffic at Woodfield Street, Morriston, August 28, 2015, the day their main use on the city's streets ended.

Windblown sand has always been a problem on roads, railways and footpaths around the bay. Excavators had been clearing the result of fierce overnight winds when this picture was taken in 2014.

Minibuses became the acknowledged salvation of the South Wales Transport company in the mid-1980s and beyond. Their 'hail and ride' services brought passengers back in their thousands. Here a line-up of different variants of those used by the company can be seen at the Quadrant bus station, mid 1990s.

A survey boat heads seaward towards the mouth of the River Tawe, just below the barrage, mid-2000s.

Bar staff are kept busy at a beer festival organised by CAMRA, the Campaign for Real Ale, held
in the Patti Pavilion and below, thirsty customers waiting to be served with their favourite ale, 1993.

Foundation work underway during construction of a new chapel at Sketty Cross, 2015.

Some of the members of the Elba and Baldwins steelworks social club, Crymlyn Burrows, enjoy the music of an accordionist, early 1950s.

Looking along Port Tennant Road, early 1920s.

Looking down over Carmarthen Road, towards Cwmfelin tinplate works and its offices, with Manselton prominent in the background, late 1940s.

A group of United Welsh busmen, drivers and conductors in front of one of the company's Albion double deckers at the Singleton Street bus station, early 1950s.

A group of dancers brave the rain and draw the crowds during a display in Oxford Street, outside the market entrance, 2014.

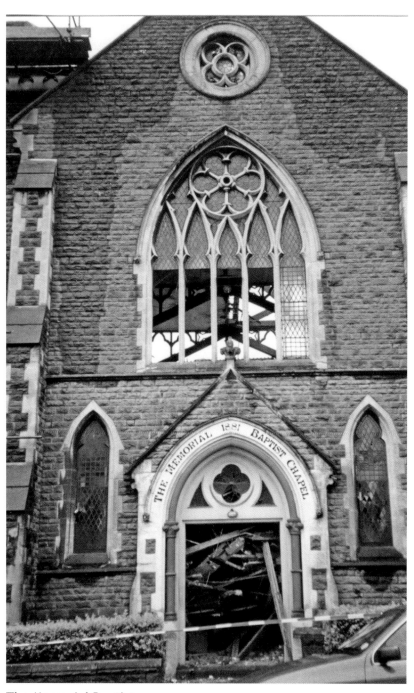

The Memorial Baptist
Chapel, Walter Road, during
its demolition, 1992.

Pupils at Danygraig
School in Welsh costume
celebrating St David's
Day, mid 1970s.

The Swansea Pilot Cutter
viewed from aboard the
MV Balmoral as it pulls
alongside to put a pilot on
board as the Balmoral
nears the mouth of the
River Tawe on a return
trip from Ilfracombe.

Children at the playground in Penclawdd on the evening of September 17, 1993, which saw the highest tide of the 20th Century.

Construction work on a new building for the Flying Angels Mission to Seamen in Swansea Docks, May 26, 1964.

A gathering of women office staff at the Co-operative House department store in Oxford Street, give a send off to one of their colleagues who was emigrating to Australia, 1964.

The junction of Princess Way and Caer Street with Castle Gardens on the left, early 1970s.

Gower Road, Sketty Cross, September 1993.

Some of the ftr metro 'Bendy buses' at rest at Ravenhill depot after their final day of operation, August, 2015.

Children of Cwmrhydyceirw School with its headteacher Arthur Rees Lewis, in the grounds of Maes y Gwernen House, Morriston at a celebration party organised and paid for by the owner of the house, Mrs Williams, to mark the Jubilee year in 1935 of King George V and Queen Mary.

A group of Sketty youngsters all dressed up for some scary Halloween antics, 1993.

Entertainer Wyn Calvin with some of his fellow cast members who took part in a show at the Empire Theatre, Christmas 1956. A year later, the theatre closed.